CONTENTS

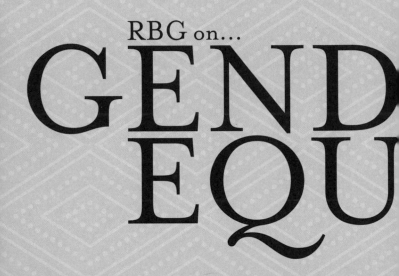

RBG on...
GENDER
EQU

ER
ALITY

"

Women will have achieved
true equality when men
share with them the
responsibility of bringing
up the next generation.

"

"

The state controlling a
woman would mean denying
her full autonomy and
full equality.

"

"

I read every federal case that had to do with women's equality or the lack thereof and every law review article. Now that seems like it was quite an undertaking but in fact, it was easily manageable because there was so little.

"

"

We should each be free
to develop our own talents,
whatever they may be,
and not be held back by
artificial barriers.

"

"

I think unconscious bias is one of the hardest things to get at. My favorite example is the symphony orchestra. When I was growing up, there were no women in orchestras. Auditioners thought they could tell the difference between a woman playing and a man...

GENDER EQUALITY

Some intelligent person devised a simple solution: Drop a curtain between the auditioners and the people trying out. And, lo and behold, women began to get jobs in symphony orchestras.

"

"

You asked me about my thinking about equal protection versus individual autonomy, and my answer to you is it's both. This is something central to a woman's life, to her dignity...

It's a decision that she must make for herself. And when Government controls that decision for her, she's being treated as less than a fully adult human responsible for her own choices.

"

"

Men and women are persons
of equal dignity and they
should count equally before
the law.

"

"

The side that wants to take
the choice away from women
and give it to the state,
they're fighting a losing
battle. Time is on the side
of change.

"

"

You can imagine how
exhilarating it was for me
when the women's movement
came alive in the late '60s
and it became possible to do
something about all that.
Before then, you were
talking to the wind...

When you think of the truly great and brave ladies, Susan B. Anthony, Elizabeth Cady Stanton, those were women who didn't have a wave to ride. We did. We came at a time when society finally was willing to listen.

"

"

The notion used to be that there were separate spheres for the sexes. Men were the doers in the world and women were the stay-at-home types.

"

"

A person's sex bears
no necessary relationship
to ability.

"

GENDER EQUALITY

"

Reproductive choice has
to be straightened out.
There will never be a woman
of means without choice
anymore. That just seems
to me so obvious…

"

"

The states that changed their
abortion laws before Roe
are not going to change
back. So we have a policy
that only affects poor
women, and it can
never be otherwise.

"

"

Feminism … I think the
simplest explanation, and one
that captures the idea, is a song
that Marlo Thomas sang, 'Free
to be You and Me.' Free to be, if
you were a girl — a doctor,
lawyer, Indian chief. Anything
you want to be. And if you're a
boy, and you like teaching, you
like nursing, you would like to
have a doll, that's OK too…

GENDER EQUALITY

That notion that we should each be free to develop our own talents, whatever they may be, and not be held back by artificial barriers — man-made barriers, certainly not heaven sent.

"

"

Young women today have
a great advantage, and it
is that there are no more
closed doors. That was
basically what the '70s was
all about. Opening doors
that had been closed to
women.

"

GENDER EQUALITY

RBG on...

SUP

THE
REME
COURT

"

People ask me sometimes…
'When will there be enough
women on the court?'
And my answer is: 'When
there are nine'.

"

THE SUPREME COURT

"

Dissents speak to a future
age. It's not simply to say,
'my colleagues are wrong
and I would do it this way,'
but the greatest dissents do
become court opinions.

"

THE SUPREME COURT

"

The notion that the
Partial-Birth Abortion Ban
Act furthers any legitimate
governmental interest is,
quite simply, irrational…

the Court's defense of it,
cannot be understood as
anything other than an
effort to chip away at a right
declared again and again by
this Court—and with increasing
comprehension of its
centrality to women's lives.

"

THE SUPREME COURT

[About being a woman on the
Supreme Court, alongside
Sandra Day O'Connor]

"

Well, it says to the world,
'We're here not as
one-at-a-time curiosities.
We are here to stay, and
in all our diversity'...

I went through the entire last
term which was my, what,
seventh year on the court,
with no one calling me Justice
O'Connor. It took six years,
but that, to me, was a sign that
we've really made it, that all
know there are two women.

99

THE SUPREME COURT

[On being the lone female
Supreme Court justice briefly]

66

It's almost like being back
in law school in 1956, when
there were nine of us in a class
of over 500, so that meant
most sections had just
two women, and you felt that
every eye was on you...

Every time you went to
answer a question, you were
answering for your entire
sex. It may not have been
true, but certainly you felt
that way. You were different
and the object of curiosity.

"

THE SUPREME COURT

"

Justices continue to think
and can change. I am ever
hopeful that if the court has
a blind spot today, its eyes
will be open tomorrow.

"

"

I was a law school teacher.
And that's how I regard
my role here with my
colleagues, who haven't
had the experience of
growing up female…

and don't fully appreciate
the arbitrary barriers
that have been put in
womens' way.

,,

THE SUPREME COURT

"

We care about this
institution more than our
individual egos and we are
all devoted to keeping the
Supreme Court in the place
that it is…

.

THE SUPREME COURT

as a co-equal third
branch of government
and I think a model for
the world in the collegiality
and independence
of judges.

99

THE SUPREME COURT

"

I'm dejected, but only momentarily, when I can't get the fifth vote for something I think is very important. But then you go on to the next challenge and you give it your all…

You know that these
important issues are
not going to go away.
They are going to come
back again and again.
There'll be another time,
another day.

"

THE SUPREME COURT

RBG on…
DISCRIM

INATION

"

We should not be held back
from pursuing our full
talents, from contributing
what we could contribute to
the society, because we fit
into a certain mold...

because we belong to
a group that historically
has been the object of
discrimination.

99

"

When a thoughtless or
unkind word is spoken, best
tune it out. Reacting in
anger or annoyance will not
advance one's ability
to persuade.

"

"

The greatest statement of
equality is in the Declaration
of Independence, written
by a slaveholder.

"

"

Just as buildings in
California have a greater
need to be earthquake
proofed...

places where there is greater
racial polarization in voting
have a greater need for
prophylactic measures to
prevent purposeful race
discrimination.

"

"

Throwing out preclearance
when it has worked and is
continuing to work to stop
discriminatory changes...

is like throwing away
your umbrella in a
rainstorm because you
are not getting wet.

,,

[On marriage equality
for everyone]

❝

All of the incentives, all
of the benefits marriage
affords would still be
available. So you're not
taking away anything from
heterosexual couples...

They would have the very
same incentive to marry,
with all the benefits that
come with marriage
that they do now.

"

"

All I can say is I am
sensitive to discrimination
on any basis because I have
experienced that upset.

"

DISCRIMINATION

RBG on...
HER

SELF

"

Every now and then it helps
to be a little deaf... That
advice has stood me in good
stead. Not simply in dealing
with my marriage, but in
dealing with my colleagues.

"

"

You can't have it all, all at once. Who—man or woman— has it all, all at once? Over my lifespan I think I have had it all. But in different periods of time things were rough.

"

"

I try to teach through
my opinions, through my
speeches, how wrong it is to
judge people on the basis of
what they look like, color of
their skin, whether they're
men or women.

"

HERSELF

"

If I had any talent
in the world…
I would be a great diva.

"

HERSELF

"

If you have a caring
life partner, you help
the other person when
that person needs it...

HERSELF

I had a life partner who
thought my work was
as important as his, and
I think that made all the
difference for me.

"

"

My mother told me two
things constantly. One was
to be a lady, and the other
was to be independent. The
study of law was unusual for
women of my generation.
For most girls growing up in
the 40s, the most important
degree was not your B.A.,
but your M.R.S.,

"

HERSELF

"

[Justice O'Connor] said
when you're up to
chemotherapy, you do it
on Friday afternoon. You'll
get over it over the weekend,
and you'll be able to come to
the court on Monday.

"

66

Work-life balance was a term
not yet coined in the years
my children were young;
and it is aptly descriptive
of the time distribution
I experienced.

99

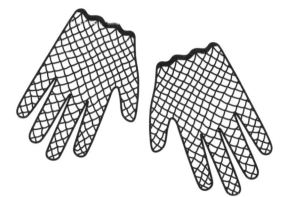

HERSELF

"

You think about what
would have happened…
suppose I had gotten a job
as a permanent associate.
Probably I would have
climbed up the ladder
and today I would be
a retired partner…

So often in life, things
that you regard as an
impediment turn out to
be great good fortune.

"

[On the Notorious
RBG Tumblr account]

"

I think a law clerk told me
about this Tumblr and also
explained to me what
'Notorious RBG' was a
parody on. And now my
grandchildren love it and
I try to keep abreast of the
latest that's on the Tumblr...

HERSELF

[I]n fact I think I gave you
a Notorious RBG [T-shirts].
I have quite a large supply.

99

"

At my advanced age –
I'm now an octogenarian
– I'm constantly amazed by
the number of people who
want to take my picture.

"

HERSELF

"

I have several times said
that the office I hold, now
for more than 23 years,
is the best and most
consuming job a lawyer
anywhere could have.

"

RBG on...
SOCI
and
CU

ETY
LTURE

"

No one who is in business for profit can foist his or her beliefs on a workforce that includes many people who do not share those beliefs.

"

"

I think our system is being
polluted by money.

"

"

Fight for the things that you
care about, but do it in a way
that will lead others to
join you.

"

SOCIETY AND CULTURE

"

I'm a very strong believer
in listening and learning
from others.

"

"

If you want to influence
people, you want them to
accept your suggestions, you
don't say, 'You don't know
how to use the English
language,' or 'How could
you make that argument?...

It will be welcomed
much more if you have
a gentle touch than if
you are aggressive.

"

"

We have the oldest written
constitution still in force
in the world, and it starts
out with three words,
'We, the people.'

"

SOCIETY AND CULTURE

"

Don't be distracted by
emotions like anger, envy,
resentment. These just zap
energy and waste time.

"

"

You can disagree without
being disagreeable.

"

"

I read Simone de Beauvoir's *Second Sex* and that was an eye-opener. So I began to think, well, maybe the law could catch up with changes in society, and that was an empowering idea…

"

"

The notion was that law was,
yes, a way to earn a living,
but also to do things that
would make life a little
better for your community.

"

"

Generally, change in
our society is incremental,
I think. Real change,
enduring change, happens
one step at a time.

"

"

Reading is the key that
opens doors to many good
things in life. Reading
shaped my dreams, and
more reading helped me
make my dreams come true.

"

SOCIETY AND CULTURE

"

We live in an age in which
the fundamental principles
to which we subscribe –
liberty, equality and justice
for all – are encountering
extraordinary challenges...

But it is also an age in
which we can join hands
with others who hold to
those principles and face
similar challenges.

"

SOURCES

Bloomberg, 12th February 2015 – pp. 38–39
CBS News, 11th January 2017 – p. 91
CNN, 17th March 2009 – p. 67
CNN, 12th October 2016 – p. 56
C-SPAN, 1st July 2009 – pp. 40–41
Economist, 14th May 2018 – p. 19
Fox News, 6th February 2012 – p. 84
Guardian, 15th September 2010 – pp. 92–93
Glamour, 15th March 2016 – pp. 70–71
Huffington Post, 1st February 2012 – p. 81
Huffington Post, 15th March 2016 – pp. 22–23,
29, 37, 66, 72–73
Huffington Post, 28th March 2016 – p. 63
Huffington Post, 2nd June 2015 – p. 80
Huffington Post, 2nd June 2016 – p. 18, 24
Huffington Post, 10th August 2016 – pp. 6,
10–11, 30–31, 46–47, 50–51, 54–55, 60, 78,
79, 86

Huffington Post, 14th October 2016 – p. 87

Huffington Post, 4th May 2018 – p. 90

Makers, 15th March 2018 – pp. 8, 88–89

Makers, 2012 – p. 9

MSNBC, 17th February 2015 – p. 62

National Geographic, 8th November 2018 – p. 48

New York Times, 22nd July 1993 – p. 7, 12–13

New York Times, 7th July 2009 – pp. 15, 20–21, 34–35, 82–83

New York Times, 1st October 2016 –p. 68

New Yorker, 11th March 2013 – p. 49

The Record; Winter 2001; Vol.56, No.1 – pp. 16–17, 22–23, 32–33, 42–43

Psychology Today, 28th May 2018 – p. 28

Washington Monthly, 25th June 2013 –pp. 52–53

Washington Post, 16th April 2015 – pp. 74–75

Yahoo! Interview, 2014 – pp. 61, 64–65

Vogue, 4th May 2018 – p. 14

Pocket RBG Wisdom

Published in 2019 by Hardie Grant Books,
an imprint of Hardie Grant Publishing

Hardie Grant Books (London)
5th & 6th Floors
52–54 Southwark Street
London SE1 1UN

Hardie Grant Books (Melbourne)
Building 1, 658 Church Street
Richmond, Victoria 3121

hardiegrantbooks.com

All rights reserved. No part of this publication may be reproduced,
stored in a retrieval system or transmitted in any form by any means,
electronic, mechanical, photocopying, recording or otherwise,
without the prior written permission of the publishers and
copyright holders.

The moral rights of the author have been asserted.

Copyright text © Hardie Grant 2019

British Library Cataloguing-in-Publication Data. A catalogue record
for this book is available from the British Library.

ISBN: 978-1-78488-287-7
10 9 8
Publishing Director: Kate Pollard
Senior Editor: Molly Ahuja
Junior Editor: Eila Purvis
Design: Jim Green
Cover Illustrator: Michele Rosenthal
Colour Reproduction by p2d
Printed and bound in China by Leo Paper Products Ltd.